# CONTENTS

# Introduction

Today we go to see the doctor whenever we feel ill. We make an **appointment** at a **health centre**, **surgery** or hospital.

Today, when you go to the doctor, there are toys and games to play with while you wait.

In the past, it was more difficult to see a doctor. There were no health centres and only a few hospitals.

In the past, there was not much for children to do in the doctor's waiting room.

TIME LINE

| 1900s | 1910s | 1920s | 1930s | 1940s |

# Going to the Doctor

Fiona Macdonald

# W
# FRANKLIN WATTS

NEW        EY

First published in 1998 by
Franklin Watts
96 Leonard Street
London EC2A 4RH

Franklin Watts Australia
14 Mars Road
Lane Cove
NSW 2006 Australia

**Editor:** Helen Lanz
**Art Director:** Robert Walster
**Designer:** Karen Lieberman
**Consultant:** Dr Andrew
Cunningham of the
Wellcome Unit, Cambridge

ISBN 0 7496 3074 4
Dewey Decimal
Classification Number:
610.69
Printed in Malaysia

**Picture Credits**

Cover images: Hulton Getty
(main image), Watts (br),
Science and Society Picture
Library (bl)

Interior: Franklin Watts pp.
7 (Chris Honeywell), 10r,
15b (Steve Shott), 19t
(Steve Shott), 25b (Chris
Honeywell), 26t & b
(Steve Shott), 28t, 29l, 29r;
Sally and Richard Greenhill
pp. 6l, 12r, 19b, 23b, 25t;
Robert Harding Picture
Library p. 10l; Hulton Getty
Collection pp. 4, 8l, 8r, 9, 11,
13, 15t 16, 17t, 18, 20, 23t, 24l,
27t; Mansell/ Time Inc. pp.
6r, 22, 27b; Robert Opie pp.
3, 17b; Rex Features pp. 12l,
14; Science and Society
Picture Library pp. 24r,
28b; Spectrum Colour
Library p. 21

Going to see the doctor today.

This book will tell you
what going to the doctor
was like many years ago.

*Look at this time line.
It will tell you when the
photographs showing
the past were taken.*

**1950s    1960s    1970s    1980s    1990s    2000s**

# Poor and ill

In the early 1900s, some people were very poor. They did not have enough money to buy food or warm clothes.

Being hungry and cold made people weak, so they often fell ill.

Boys in London around 1900. Their clothes are ragged and one of them has no shoes.

Some poor families could not afford to feed their children with healthy food.

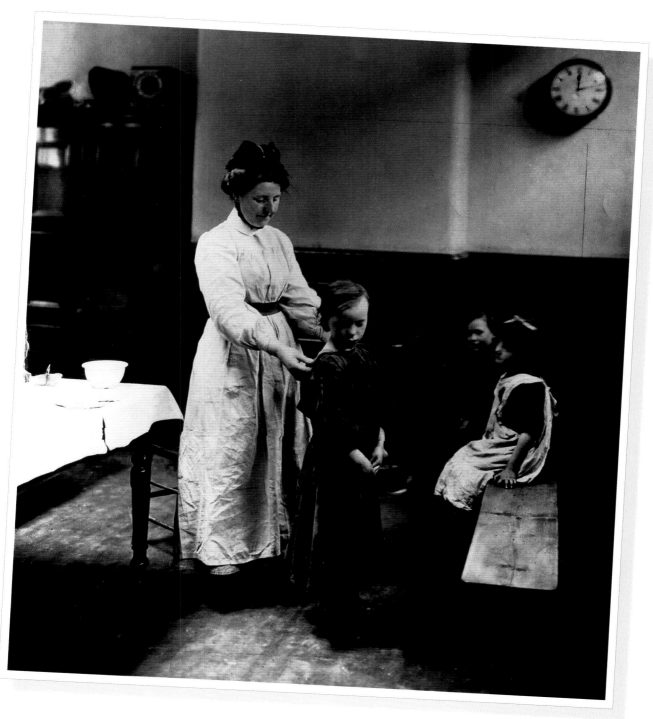

In the early 1900s, there were some
hospitals that cared especially for poor people.

# Ambulances

When an accident happens, injured people need to see a doctor quickly!

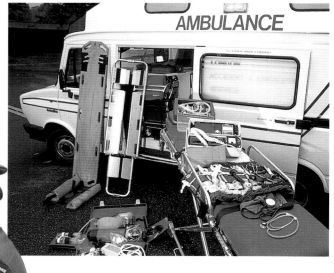

This modern ambulance has a powerful engine. It carries a lot of life-saving *equipment.*

Today, an **ambulance** can rush them to hospital at high speed.

Two ambulancemen lift a patient on a stretcher.

TIME LINE

1900s   **1910s**   1920s   1930s   1940s

A nurse, dressed in white, helps to lift an injured man into a horse-drawn ambulance in about 1910.

In the past, ambulances were much slower. They were pulled by horses and did not move very fast.

# Scanners and x-rays

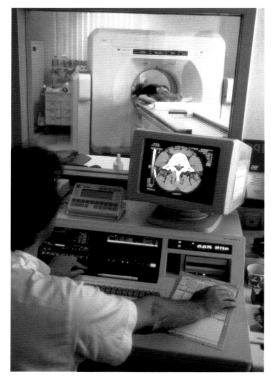

Scanners show the pictures on computer screens.

Today, doctors use scanners to see inside people's bodies. Scanners show pictures of bones, muscles, hearts, lungs and brains.

Doctors also use **x-rays** to see inside people's bodies.

A doctor looks at an x-ray picture today.

In the past, doctors could only take x-ray pictures. X-ray machines took good pictures of broken bones, but did not show other parts of the body very clearly.

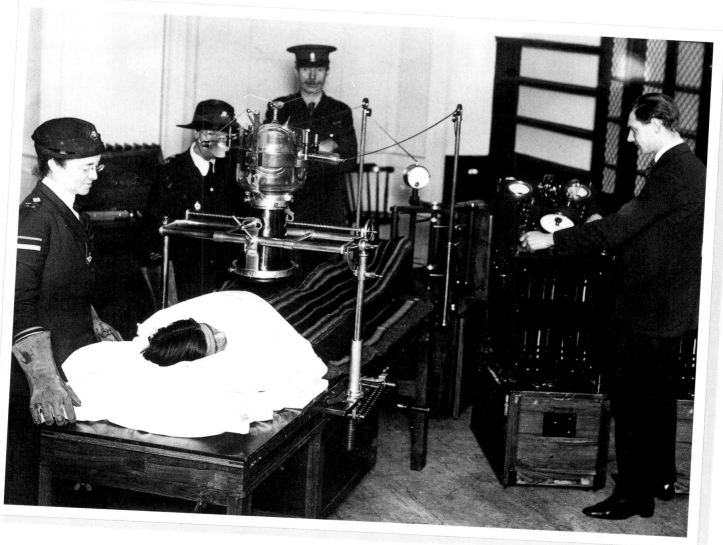

A patient being x-rayed in 1921.

# Plasters and splints

In the past, doctors put broken bones in plaster to keep them straight while they grew together again.

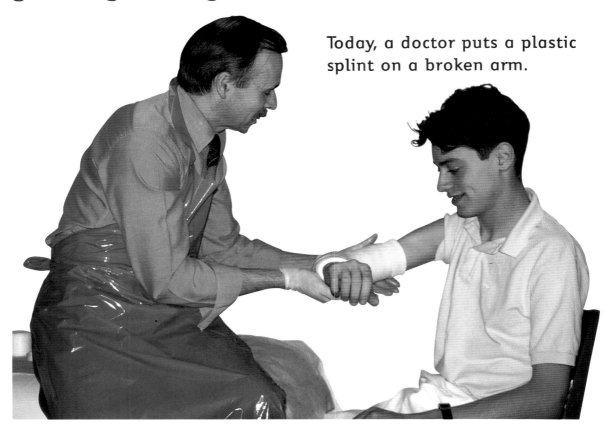

Today, a doctor puts a plastic splint on a broken arm.

Today doctors still use plaster to keep broken bones straight. But sometimes doctors use plastic **splints**, instead.

TIME LINE

1900s    1910s    **1920s**    1930s    1940s

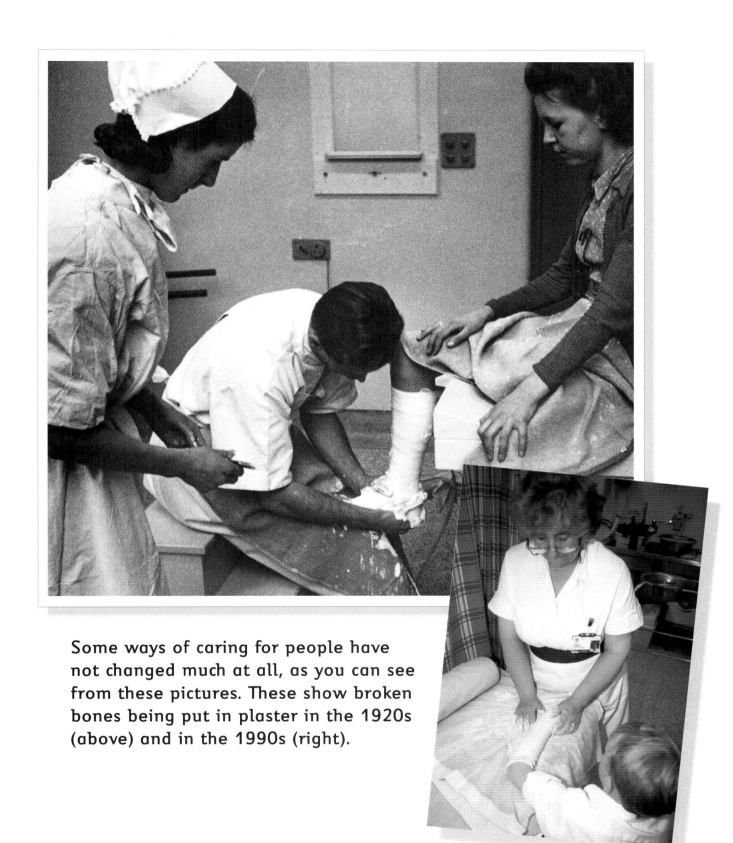

Some ways of caring for people have not changed much at all, as you can see from these pictures. These show broken bones being put in plaster in the 1920s (above) and in the 1990s (right).

# The chemist's shop

In the past, people paid to see the doctor.
They paid for all the **medicines** he gave them, too.

If people did not have enough money to see the
doctor, they went to a **chemist's** shop, instead.

A chemist's shop in the 1920s.

These women were all trained chemists. In the 1920s and 1930s they made their own medicines to sell.

Chemists gave free advice. Medicines were often much cheaper from the chemist than from the doctor.

In the past, bottles of medicine were made of glass and had cork stoppers.

# In hospital

In the past, children's **wards** were dull
and gloomy. There was not much to do.

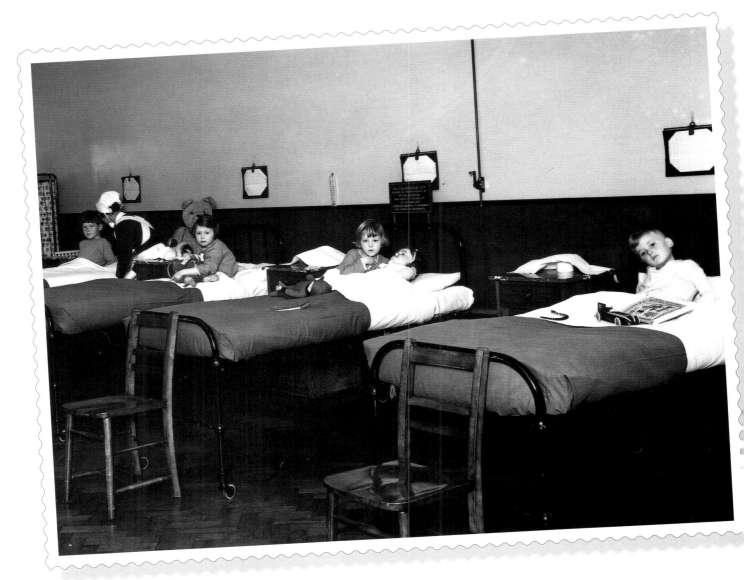

Children in hospital in the 1930s. They
often had to spend many hours in bed.

TIME LINE

1900s    1910s    1920s    **1930s**    1940s

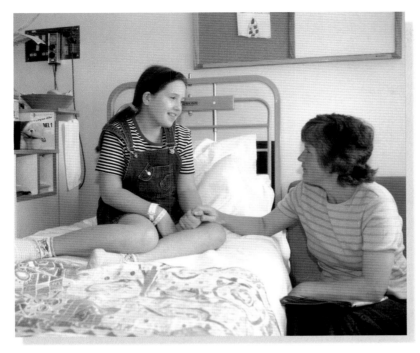

Today, hospital wards for children are bright and cheerful. There is always lots for the children to do.

Today, a busy ward with plenty of light helps to make the patients feel better.

Nurses and special hospital teachers help children to learn and play.

# Dangerous diseases

Sometimes doctors cannot **cure** dangerous **diseases**. In the past, to stop diseases from spreading, doctors used to send patients to special hospitals.

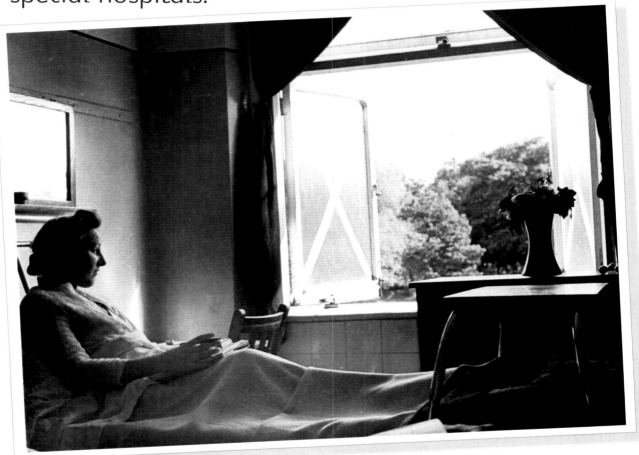

In 1942, this sick woman was put in a hospital room all by herself. This was so other people would not catch her germs.

TIME LINE

1900s    1910s    1920s    1930s    **1940s**

Doctors told people who were ill to rest, eat good food, and breathe lots of fresh air.

Sometimes this worked, but often people did not get better, or died.

Today, doctors give sick people special medicines, called *antibiotics*. Although they can be dangerous, antibiotics can cure many diseases.

1950s    1960s    1970s    1980s    1990s    2000s

# Mothers and babies

In the past, some mothers did not have enough money to take their babies to the doctor.
So nurses set up special **clinics** (baby-care centres).
The clinics were free.

Nurses kept careful records of each baby's height and weight to make sure that it was growing properly.

A mother helps to feed babies at a baby clinic in the late 1940s.

TIME LINE

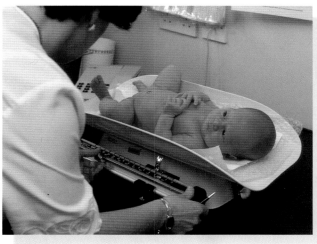

In 1944, nurses at a clinic used scales with brass weights to see how much a baby weighed. Today, the way babies are weighed has changed!

1950s    1960s    1970s    1980s    1990s    2000s

# Home visits

A nurse visits a sick baby at home in the 1950s.

Some equipment that doctors and nurses carry with them, like this stethoscope from the 1950s, has not changed much today. A stethoscope is used to listen to people's heart beats.

In the past, doctors and nurses visited very sick people at home.

They carried their medicines and equipment in a big black bag.

Today, doctors and nurses still make home visits. They take mobile phones and **pagers** with them. But they still carry the things they need for treating patients in a big black bag!

A doctor's black bag today. Doctors now have a lot more equipment to carry around with them than doctors in the past.

# Getting better

People sometimes feel weak and tired after they have been ill. Doctors, nurses and specially-trained teachers, called **physiotherapists**, help them to do exercises so they feel strong and healthy again.

Today, many hospitals have their own gyms. Patients can use the equipment to help them build up their strength.

Doing exercises with a physiotherapist in a hospital pool.

TIME LINE

1900s    1910s    1920s    1930s    1940s

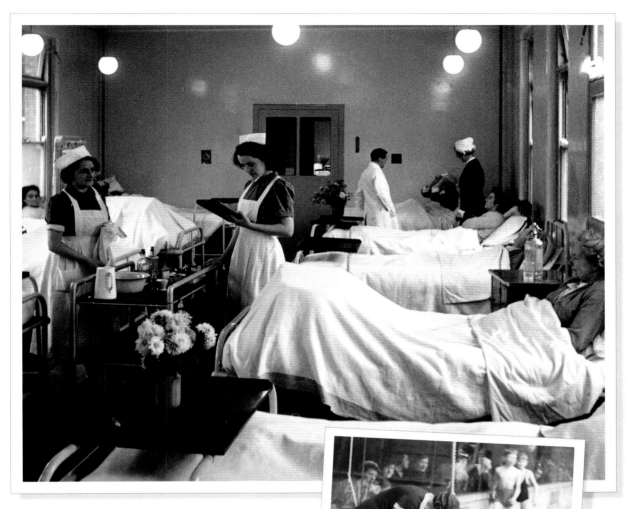

Getting better in the 1950s. Resting in bed (above) was thought to be a good way to get better.

Some patients did exercises in a hospital pool (right), but they didn't get as much help as today.

# Useful words

**ambulance:** a vehicle for taking sick and injured people to hospital.

**antibiotic:** medicine that doctors give people to cure certain diseases.

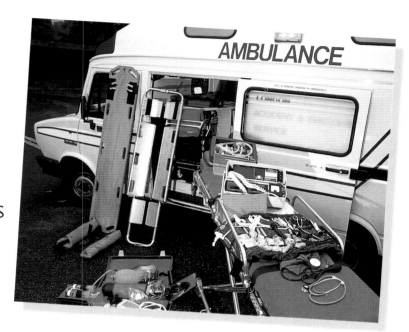

**appointment:** a meeting arranged for a certain time.

**clinic:** a place where people go for special health-care.

**chemists:** (1) specially-trained men and women who make and sell medicines (2) shops where you can buy medicines, and things like soap, toothpaste and shampoo.

**cure:** to make people well again.

**disease:** an illness.

**equipment:** things that are needed to do a job.

**health centre:** a place where doctors and nurses care for people.

**medicines:** pills or injections, for example, that a doctor or chemist gives people to make them feel better.

**pager:** a machine that makes a bleeping noise to let the person know that someone is trying to speak to them.

**physiotherapist:** someone who teaches people special exercises to help them get better.

**splints:** pieces of plastic that hold broken bones in the right place so that they mend properly.

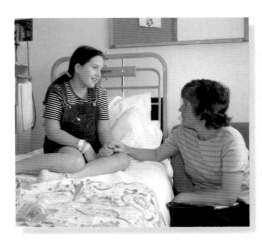

**surgery:** a place where people see a doctor or nurse.

**ward:** a room in a hospital with beds for the patients.

**x-rays:** invisible rays that can take pictures of bones.

# Index